...ille, Tennessee, by Thomas Nelson. Thomas Nelson
...stered trademark of Thomas Nelson, Inc.

...ssociation with Yates & Yates, www.yates2.com

...nc., titles may be purchased in bulk for educational,
...aising, or sales promotional use. For information,
...mail SpecialMarkets@ThomasNelson.com.

...erwise noted, Scripture quotations are from
...ING JAMES VERSION of the Bible. © 1979,
...1982, Thomas Nelson, Inc., Publishers.

...ions noted NIV are from the HOLY BIBLE: NEW
...'ERSION®. © 1973, 1978, 1984 by International Bible
...ssion of Zondervan Publishing House. All rights reserved.

...vere previously published in *The Winning Attitude, Failing*
...*p for Success, The 17 Indisputable Laws of Teamwork, and*
...*he 21 Irrefutable Laws of Leadership.*

...**Congress Cataloging-in-Publication Data**

Maxwell, John C., 1947–
...Attitude 101 /, John C. Maxwell.
p. cm.
ISBN 978-0-7852-6350-0
...hological aspects. 2. Attitude (Psychology). I. Title.
BF637.S8 M3415 2002
153.8'5—dc21
2002011491

...rinted in the United States of America

09 10 11 12 WOR 30 29 28 27

A

1

WHA

JO

NASHVILLE I

Scripture quot
INTERNATIONAL
Society. Used by perm

Portions of this book
Forward, Your Roadm

Library

1. Success—Ps

CONTENTS

Publisher's Preface

Who cares about a person's attitude? As long as someone can do the job, you shouldn't worry too much about it, right? If John Maxwell believed that, you wouldn't have *Attitude 101* in your hands right now.

As America's leadership expert, Dr. Maxwell has devoted his life to helping people become more successful. His books and seminars teach that anyone can be a REAL success if they master skills in four areas: Relationships, Equipping, Attitude, and Leadership. This book is designed to give you the essentials of attitude—in a quick, easy-to-read format.

People's lives are so hectic. Their time is valuable, and yet, they are also on information overload. More new information has been produced in the last thirty years than in the previous five thousand. A weekday edition of the *New York Times* contains more information than average people in seventeenth-century England were likely to come across in their lifetime. The amount of information available in the world has doubled in the last five years, and it will keep doubling.

So this book, a companion to *Leadership 101*, *Relationships 101* (available January 2004), and *Equipping 101* (available January 2004), is the short course on attitude. Dr. Maxwell recognizes that as an individual, your attitude has a profound impact on your life. As a leader, you cannot ignore the attitudes of the people you lead and expect to achieve success—whether you're leading a business, a family, a sports team, or a group of volunteers. A person's attitude impacts their relationships, colors their view of failure, and defines their approach to success. Attitude can make or break you.

We are delighted to publish *Attitude 101* because we realize that few things in life are a greater asset than an attitude of positive determination. *Attitude 101* is designed to empower you and your team to succeed by helping you become equipped with the right kind of attitude. Here's to your success—and to your reaching the next level!

PART I

THE IMPACT OF ATTITUDE

I

How Does Attitude Impact
Leadership?

Attitude is always a "player" on your team.

Growing up, I loved basketball. It all started for me in the fourth grade when I saw a high school basketball game for the first time. I was captivated. After that, I could usually be found practicing my shooting and playing pickup games on my small court at home.

By the time I got to high school, I had become a pretty good player. I started on the junior varsity team as a freshman, and when I was a sophomore, our JV team had a 15-3 record, which was better than that of the varsity. We were proud of our performance—maybe a little too proud.

The next year, critics who followed high school basketball in Ohio thought our team had a chance to win the state championship in our division. I guess they looked at the players who would return as seniors from the previous year's varsity team, saw the talent that would be moving up from the JV, and figured we would be a powerhouse. And we did have

1

a lot of talent. How many high school teams in the late 1960s could say that all but a couple of players on the team could dunk the ball? But the season turned out far different from everyone's expectations.

FROM BAD TO WORSE

From the beginning of the season, the team suffered problems. There were two of us juniors on the varsity who had the talent to start for the team: John Thomas, who was the team's best rebounder, and me, the best shooting guard. We thought playing time should be based strictly on ability, and we figured we deserved our place on the team. The seniors, who had taken a backseat to the previous year's seniors, thought we should be made to pay our dues and wait on the bench.

What began as a rivalry between the JV and varsity the year before turned into a war between the juniors and the seniors. When we scrimmaged at practice, it was the juniors against the seniors. In games the seniors wouldn't pass to the juniors and vice versa. The battles became so fierce that before long, the juniors and the seniors wouldn't even work together on the court during games. Our coach, Don Neff, had to platoon us. The seniors would start, and when a substitution became necessary, he'd put not one but five juniors in the game. We became two teams on one roster.

I don't remember exactly who started the rivalry that split our team, but I do remember that John Thomas and I embraced it early on. I've always been a leader, and I did my share of influencing other team members. Unfortunately, I have to confess that I led the juniors in the wrong direction.

What started as a bad attitude in one or two players made a mess of the situation for everyone. By the time we were in the thick of our schedule, even the players who didn't want to take part in the rivalry were affected. The season was a disaster. In the end, we finished with a mediocre record and never came close to reaching our potential. It just goes to show you, rotten attitudes ruin a team.

TALENT IS NOT ENOUGH

From my high school basketball experience I learned that talent is not enough to bring success to a team. Of course, you need talent. My friend Lou Holtz, the outstanding college football coach, observed, "You've got to have great athletes to win . . . You can't win without good athletes, but you can lose with them." But it also takes much more than talented people to win.

My high school teammates were loaded with talent, and if that were enough, we could have been state champions. But we were also loaded with rotten attitudes. You know which won the battle between talent and attitude in the end. Perhaps that is why to this day I understand the importance of a positive attitude and have placed such a strong emphasis on it for myself, for my children as they were growing up, and for the teams I lead.

Years ago I wrote something about attitude for my book *The Winning Attitude*. I'd like to share it with you:

> Attitude . . .
> It is the "advance man" of our true selves.
> Its roots are inward but its fruit is outward.
> It is our best friend or our worst enemy.
> It is more honest and more consistent than our words.
> It is an outward look based on past experiences.
> It is a thing which draws people to us or repels them.
> It is never content until it is expressed.
> It is the librarian of our past.
> It is the speaker of our present.
> It is the prophet of our future.[1]

Good attitudes among players do not guarantee a team's success, but bad attitudes guarantee its failure. The following five truths about attitudes clarify how they affect teamwork and a leader's team:

1. Attitudes Have the Power to Lift Up or Tear Down a Team

In *The Winner's Edge* Denis Waitley stated, "The real leaders in business, in the professional community, in education, in government, and in the home also seem to draw upon a special cutting edge that separates them from the rest of society. The winner's edge is not in a gifted birth, in a high IQ, or in talent. The winner's edge is in the attitude, not aptitude."[2]

Unfortunately, I think too many people resist that notion. They want to believe that talent alone (or talent with experience) is enough. But plenty of talented teams out there never amount to anything because of the attitudes of their players.

Various attitudes may impact a team made up of highly talented players:

Abilities	+	Attitudes	=	Result
Great Talent	+	Rotten Attitudes	=	Bad Team
Great Talent	+	Bad Attitudes	=	Average Team
Great Talent	+	Average Attitudes	=	Good Team
Great Talent	+	Good Attitudes	=	Great Team

If you want outstanding results, you need good people with great talent and awesome attitudes. When attitudes go up, so does the potential of the team. When attitudes go down, the potential of the team goes with it.

2. AN ATTITUDE COMPOUNDS WHEN EXPOSED TO OTHERS

Several things on a team are not contagious: talent, experience, and willingness to practice. But you can be sure of one thing: Attitude is catching. When someone on the team is teachable and his humility is rewarded by improvement, others are more likely to display similar characteristics. When a leader is upbeat in the face of discouraging circumstances, others admire that quality and want to be like her. When a team member displays a strong work ethic and begins to have a positive impact, others imitate him. People become inspired by their peers. People have a tendency to adopt the attitudes of those they spend time with—to pick up on their mind-sets, beliefs, and approaches to challenges.

The story of Roger Bannister is an inspiring example of the way attitudes often "compound." During the first half of the twentieth century, many sports experts believed that no runner could run a mile in less than four minutes. And for a long time they were right. But then on May 6, 1954, British runner and university student Roger Bannister ran a mile in 3 minutes 59.4 seconds during a meet in Oxford. Less than two months later, another runner, Australian John Landy, also broke the four-minute barrier. Then suddenly dozens and then hundreds of others broke it. Why? Because the best runners' attitudes changed. They began to adopt the mind-sets and beliefs of their peers.

Bannister's attitude and actions compounded when exposed to others. His attitude spread. Today, every world-class runner who competes at that distance can run a mile in less than four minutes. Attitudes are contagious!

3. Bad Attitudes Compound Faster Than Good Ones

There's only one thing more contagious than a good attitude—a bad attitude. For some reason many people think it's chic to be negative. I suspect that they think it makes them appear smart or important. But the truth is that a negative attitude hurts rather than helps the person who has it. And it also hurts the people around him.

To see how quickly and easily an attitude or mind-set can spread, just think about this story from Norman Cousins: Once during a football game, a doctor at the first aid station treated five people for what he suspected might be food poisoning. He soon discovered that all five people had bought drinks from a particular concession stand at the stadium.

The physician requested that the announcer advise people in the stadium to avoid buying drinks from the particular vendor because of the possibility of food poisoning. Before long, more than two hundred people complained of food poisoning symptoms. Nearly half the people's symptoms were so severe that they were taken to the hospital.

The story doesn't end there, however. After a little more

detective work, it was discovered that the five original victims had eaten tainted potato salad from one particular deli on the way to the game. When the other "sufferers" found out that the drinks in the stadium were safe, they experienced miraculous recoveries. That just goes to show you, an attitude spreads very quickly.

4. ATTITUDES ARE SUBJECTIVE, SO IDENTIFYING A WRONG ONE CAN BE DIFFICULT

Have you ever interacted with someone for the first time and suspected that his attitude was poor, yet you were unable to put your finger on exactly what was wrong? I believe many people have that experience.

ATTITUDE IS REALLY ABOUT HOW A PERSON IS. THAT OVERFLOWS INTO HOW HE ACTS.

The reason people doubt their observations about others' attitudes is that attitudes are subjective. Someone with a bad attitude may not do anything illegal or unethical, yet his attitude may be ruining the team just the same.

People always project on the outside how they feel on the inside. Attitude is really about how a person is. That overflows into how he acts. Allow me to share with you common rotten attitudes that ruin a team so that you can recognize them for what they are when you see them.

An inability to admit wrongdoing. Have you ever spent time with people who never admit they're wrong? It's painful. Nobody's perfect, but someone who thinks he is does not make an ideal teammate. His wrong attitude will always create conflict.

Failing to forgive. It's said that Clara Barton, the founder of modern nursing, was once encouraged to bemoan a cruel act inflicted on her years earlier, but Barton wouldn't take the bait.

"Don't you remember the wrong that was done to you?" the friend goaded.

"No," answered Barton, "I distinctly remember forgetting that."

Holding a grudge is never positive or appropriate. And when unforgiveness occurs between teammates, it's certain to hurt the team.

Petty jealousy. An attitude that really works against people is the desire for equality that feeds petty jealousy. For some reason the people with this attitude believe that every person deserves equal treatment, regardless of talent, performance, or impact. Yet nothing could be farther from the truth. Each of us is created uniquely and performs differently, and as a result, we should be treated as such.

The disease of me. In his book *The Winner Within*, highly successful NBA coach Pat Riley writes about the "disease of me." He says of team members who have it, "They develop an overpowering belief in their own importance. Their actions virtually shout the claim, 'I'm the one.'" Riley asserts that the disease always has the same inevitable result: "The Defeat of Us."[3]

A critical spirit. Fred and Martha were driving home after a church service. "Fred," Martha asked, "did you notice that the pastor's sermon was kind of weak today?"

"No, not really," answered Fred.

"Well, did you hear that the choir was flat?"

"No, I didn't," he responded.

"Well, you certainly must have noticed that young couple and their children right in front of us, with all the noise and commotion they made the whole service!"

"I'm sorry, dear, but no, I didn't."

Finally in disgust Martha said, "Honestly, Fred, I don't know why you even bother to go to church."

When someone on the team has a critical spirit, everybody knows it because everyone on the team can do no right.

A desire to hog all the credit. Another bad attitude that hurts the team is similar to the "disease of me." But where the person with that disease may simmer in the background and create dissension, the credit hog continually steps into the spotlight to take a bow—whether he has earned it or not. His attitude is opposite that of NBA Hall of Fame center Bill

Russell, who said of his time on the court, "The most important measure of how good a game I played was how much better I'd made my teammates play."

Certainly there are other negative attitudes that I haven't named, but my intention isn't to list every bad attitude—just some of the most common ones. In a word, most bad attitudes are the result of selfishness. If one of your teammates puts others down, sabotages teamwork, or makes himself out to be more important than the team, then you can be sure that you've encountered someone with a bad attitude.

5. Rotten Attitudes, Left Alone, Ruin Everything

Bad attitudes must be addressed. You can be sure that they will always cause dissension, resentment, combativeness, and division on a team. And they will never go away on their own if they are left unaddressed. They will simply fester and ruin a team—along with its chances of reaching its potential.

Because people with bad attitudes are so difficult to deal with and because attitudes seem so subjective, you may doubt your gut reaction when you encounter someone with a bad attitude. After all, if it's only your opinion that he has a rotten attitude, then you have no right to address it, right? Not if you care about the team. Rotten attitudes ruin a team. That is always true. If you leave a bad apple in a barrel of good apples, you will always end up with a barrel of rotten apples. Attitudes always impact a leader's effectiveness.

President Thomas Jefferson remarked, "Nothing can stop the man with the right mental attitude from achieving his goal; nothing on earth can help the man with the wrong mental attitude." If you care about your team and you are committed to helping all of the players, you can't ignore a bad attitude.

Dealing with a person whose attitude is bad can be a very tricky thing. Before you try to address the issue, you would benefit from a closer look at attitudes and how they affect an individual.

2

How Does Attitude Impact an Individual?

Your attitude and your potential go hand in hand.

What is attitude? How do you put your finger on it? Well, attitude is an inward feeling expressed by behavior. That is why an attitude can be seen without a word being said. Haven't we all noticed "the pout" of the sulker, or the "jutted jaw" of the determined? Of all the things we wear, our expression is the most important.

Sometimes our attitude can be masked outwardly and others who see us are fooled. But usually the cover-ups will not last long. There is that constant struggle as the attitude tries to wiggle its way out.

My father enjoys telling the story of the four-year-old who had one of those trouble-filled days. After reprimanding him, his mother finally said to him, "Son, you go over to that chair and sit on it now!" The little lad went to the chair, sat down and said, "Mommy, I'm sitting on the outside, but I'm standing up on the inside."

Psychologist/philosopher James Allen states, "A person cannot travel within and stand still without." Soon what is happening within us will affect what is happening without. A hardened attitude is a dreaded disease. It causes a closed mind and a dark future. When our attitude is positive and conducive to growth, the mind expands and the progress begins.

ATTITUDE DETERMINES SUCCESS OR FAILURE

While leading a conference in South Carolina, I tried the following experiment. I asked the audience, "What word describes what will determine our happiness, acceptance, peace, and success?" The audience began to express words such as *job, education, money, time.* Finally someone said *attitude.* Such an important area of their lives was a second thought. Our attitude is the primary force that will determine whether we succeed or fail.

For some, attitude presents a difficulty in every opportunity; for others it presents an opportunity in every difficulty. Some climb with a positive attitude, while others fall with a negative perspective. The very fact that the attitude "makes some" while "breaking others" is significant enough for us to explore its importance. Here are seven axioms about attitude to help you better understand how it impacts a person's life:

Attitude Axiom #1: Our Attitude Determines Our Approach to Life

Our attitude tells us what we expect from life. Like an airplane, if our "nose" is pointed up, we are taking off; if it is pointed down, we may be headed for a crash.

One of my favorite stories is about a grandpa and grandma who visited their grandchildren. Each afternoon Grandpa would lie down for a nap. One day, as a practical joke, the kids decided to put Limburger cheese in his mustache. Quite soon he awoke sniffing. "Why, this room stinks," he exclaimed as he got up and went out into the kitchen. He wasn't there long until he decided that the kitchen smelled too, so he walked outdoors for a breath of fresh air. Much to Grandpa's surprise, the open air brought no relief, and he proclaimed, "The whole world stinks!"

How true that is to life! When we carry "Limburger cheese" in our attitudes, the whole world smells bad. We are individually responsible for our view of life. That truth has been known for ages and is contained in Scripture: "For whatever a man sows, that he will also reap."[1] Our attitude toward and action in life help determine what happens to us.

It would be impossible to estimate the number of jobs lost, the number of promotions missed, the number of sales not made, and the number of marriages ruined by poor attitudes.

But almost daily we witness jobs that are held but hated and marriages that are tolerated but unhappy, all because people are waiting for others, or the world, to change instead of realizing that they are responsible for their own behavior.

ATTITUDE AXIOM #2: OUR ATTITUDE DETERMINES OUR RELATIONSHIPS WITH PEOPLE

All of life is impacted by your relationships with people, yet establishing relationships is difficult. You can't get along with some people, and you can't make it without them. That's why it is essential to build proper relationships with others in our crowded world.

The Stanford Research Institute says that the money you make in any endeavor is determined only 12.5 percent by knowledge and 87.5 percent by your ability to deal with people.

87.5% people knowledge + 12.5% product knowledge = Success

That is why Teddy Roosevelt said, "The most important single ingredient to the formula of success is knowing how to get along with people." And why John D. Rockefeller said, "I will pay more for the ability to deal with people than any other ability under the sun."

When the attitude we possess places others first and we see people as important, then our perspective will reflect their viewpoint, not ours. Until we walk in the other person's shoes and see life through another's eyes, we will be like the man who angrily jumped out of his car after a collision with another car. "Why don't you people watch where you're driving?" he shouted wildly. "You're the fourth car I've hit today!"

Usually the person who rises within an organization has a good attitude. The promotions did not give that individual an outstanding attitude, but an outstanding attitude resulted in promotions.

Attitude Axiom #3: Often Our Attitude Is the Only Difference Between Success and Failure

History's greatest achievements have been made by men who excelled only slightly over the masses of others in their fields. This could be called the principle of the slight edge. Many times that slight difference was attitude. The former Israeli Prime Minister Golda Meir underlined this truth in one of her interviews. She said, "All my country has is spirit. We don't have petroleum dollars. We don't have mines of great wealth in the ground. We don't have the support of a worldwide public opinion that looks favorably on us. All Israel has is the spirit of its people. And if the people lose their spirit, even the United States of America cannot save us."

Certainly aptitude is important to our success in life. Yet success or failure in any undertaking is caused more by mental attitude than by mere mental capacities. I remember times when Margaret, my wife, would come home from teaching school frustrated because of modern education's emphasis on aptitude instead of attitude. She wanted the kids to be tested on A.Q. (attitude quotient) instead of just the I.Q. (intelligence quotient). She would talk of kids whose I.Q. was high yet their performance was low. There were others whose I.Q. was low but their performance was high.

As a parent, I hope my children have excellent minds and outstanding attitudes. But if I had to choose an "either-or" situation, without hesitation I would want their A.Q. to be high.

A Yale University president some years ago gave similar advice to a former president of Ohio State: "Always be kind to your A and B students. Someday one of them will return to your campus as a good professor. And also be kind to your C students. Someday one of them will return and build a two-million-dollar science laboratory."

There is very little difference in people, but that little difference makes a big difference. The little difference is attitude. The big difference is whether it is positive or negative.

ATTITUDE AXIOM #4: OUR ATTITUDE AT THE BEGINNING
OF A TASK WILL AFFECT ITS OUTCOME MORE THAN
ANYTHING ELSE

Coaches understand the importance of their teams' having the right attitude before facing a tough opponent. Surgeons want to see their patients mentally prepared before going into surgery. Job-seekers know that their prospective employer is looking for more than just skills when they apply for work. Public speakers want a conducive atmosphere before they communicate to their audience. Why? Because the right attitude in the beginning ensures success at the end. You are acquainted with the saying "All's well that ends well." An equal truth is "All's well that begins well."

Most projects fail or succeed before they begin. A young mountain climber and an experienced guide were ascending a high peak in the Sierras. Early one morning the young climber was suddenly awakened by a tremendous cracking sound. He was convinced that the end of the world had come. The guide responded, "It's not the end of the world, just the dawning of a new day." As the sun rose, it was merely hitting the ice and causing it to melt.

Many times we have been guilty of viewing our future challenges as the sunset of life rather than the sunrise of a bright new opportunity.

For instance, there's the story of two shoe salesmen who were sent to an island to sell shoes. The first salesman, upon arrival, was shocked to realize that no one wore shoes. Immediately he sent a telegram to his home office in Chicago saying, "Will return home tomorrow. No one wears shoes."

The second salesman was thrilled by the same realization. Immediately he wired the home office in Chicago saying, "Please send me 10,000 shoes. Everyone here needs them."

ATTITUDE AXIOM #5: OUR ATTITUDE CAN TURN OUR PROBLEMS INTO BLESSINGS

In *Awake, My Heart,* J. Sidlow Baxter wrote, "What is the difference between an obstacle and an opportunity? Our attitude toward it. Every opportunity has a difficulty and every difficulty has an opportunity."[2]

When confronted with a difficult situation, a person with an outstanding attitude makes the best of it while he gets the worst of it. Life can be likened to a grindstone. Whether it grinds you down or polishes you depends upon what you are made of.

While attending a conference of young leaders, I heard this statement: "No society has ever developed tough men during times of peace." Adversity is prosperity to those who possess a great attitude. Kites rise against, not with, the wind. When the adverse wind of criticism blows, allow it to be to you what the blast of wind is to the kite—a force against it that lifts it higher. A kite would not fly unless it had the controlling tension of the string to tie it down. It is equally true in life. Consider the following successes that were accomplished through a positive attitude.

WHEN CONFRONTED WITH A DIFFICULT SITUATION, A PERSON WITH AN OUTSTANDING ATTITUDE MAKES THE BEST OF IT WHILE HE GETS THE WORST OF IT.

When Napoleon's school companions made sport of him because of his humble origin and poverty, he devoted himself entirely to his books. Quickly rising above his classmates in scholarship, he commanded their respect. Soon he was regarded as the brightest in the class.

Few people knew Abraham Lincoln until the great weight of the Civil War showed his character.

Robinson Crusoe was written in prison. John Bunyan wrote *Pilgrim's Progress* in the Bedford jail. Sir Walter Raleigh wrote *The History of the World* during a thirteen-year imprisonment. Luther translated the Bible while confined in the castle of Wartburg. For ten years Dante, author of *The Divine Comedy*, worked in exile and under the sentence of death. Beethoven was almost totally deaf and burdened with sorrow when he produced his greatest works.

When God wants to educate someone, He does not send

him to the school of graces but to the school of necessities. Great leaders emerge when crises occur. In the lives of people who achieve, we read repeatedly of terrible troubles that forced them to rise above the commonplace. Not only do they find the answers, but they also discover a tremendous power within themselves. Like a groundswell far out in the ocean, this force within explodes into a mighty wave when circumstances seem to overcome. Then out steps the athlete, the author, the statesman, the scientist, or the businessman. David Sarnoff said, "There is plenty of security in the cemetery; I long for opportunity."

ATTITUDE AXIOM #6: OUR ATTITUDE CAN GIVE US AN UNCOMMONLY POSITIVE PERSPECTIVE

An uncommonly positive perspective is able to help us accomplish some uncommon goals. I have keenly observed the different approaches and results achieved by a positive thinker and by a person filled with fear and apprehension. For example, in ancient Israel when Goliath came up against the Hebrews, the soldiers all thought, *He's so big we can never kill him.* David looked at the same giant and thought, *He's so big I can't miss.*

George Sweeting, former president of Moody Bible Institute, tells a story about a Scotsman who was an extremely hard worker and expected all the men under him to be the same. His men would tease him, "Scotty, don't you know that Rome wasn't built in a day?" "Yes," he would answer, "I know that. But I wasn't foreman on that job."

Individuals whose attitudes cause them to approach life from an entirely positive perspective are not always understood. They are what some would call a "no-limit people." In other words, they don't accept the normal limitations of life as most people do. They are unwilling to accept "the accepted" just because it is accepted. Their response to self-limiting conditions will probably be "why?" instead of "okay." Certainly, they have limitations. Their gifts are not so plentiful that they cannot fail. But they are determined to walk to the very edge of their potential and the potential of their goals before accepting defeat.

They are like bumblebees. According to a theory of aerodynamics, as demonstrated through the wind tunnel tests, the bumblebee should be unable to fly. Because of the size, weight, and shape of its body in relationship to the total wing span, flying is scientifically impossible. The bumblebee, being ignorant of scientific theory, goes ahead and flies anyway and makes honey every day.

The future not only looks bright when the attitude is right, but also the present is much more enjoyable. The positive person understands that the journey of success is as enjoyable as the destination. Asked which of his works he would select as his masterpiece, architect Frank Lloyd Wright, at the age of eighty-three, replied, "My next one."

A friend of mine in Ohio drove eighteen-wheelers for an interstate trucking company. Knowing the hundreds of miles he logged weekly, I once asked him how he kept from getting extremely tired. "It's all in your attitude," he replied. "Some drivers 'go to work' in the morning, but I 'go for a ride in the country.'" That kind of positive perspective gives him the "edge" on life.

ATTITUDE AXIOM #7: YOUR ATTITUDE IS NOT AUTOMATICALLY GOOD BECAUSE YOU ARE A RELIGIOUS PERSON

It is noteworthy that the seven deadly sins—pride, covetousness, lust, envy, anger, gluttony, and sloth—are all matters of attitude, inner spirit, and motives. Sadly, many people of faith carry with them inner-spirit problems. They are like the elder brother contained in the parable of the prodigal son, thinking that they do everything right. While the younger brother left home to live a wild life, the elder brother chose to stay home with his father. He wasn't going to spend *his* time sowing wild oats! Yet, when the younger brother returned home, some of the elder brother's wrong attitudes began to surface.

First was a feeling of self-importance. The elder brother

was out in the field doing what he ought to do, but he got mad when the party began at home—his father would never let him have one for himself!

That was followed by a feeling of self-pity. The elder brother said, "Look! For so many years I have been serving you, and you have never thrown a party for me. But when your son who wasted all of your money comes home, you give him a big celebration."[3]

Often people overlook the true meaning of the story of the prodigal son. They forget that there are not one but two prodigals. The younger brother is guilty of the sins of the flesh, whereas the elder brother is guilty of the sins of the spirit. His problem is his attitude. At the end of the parable, it is the elder brother—the second prodigal—who is outside the father's house.

And that is a good lesson for all of us to remember. A poor attitude will take us places we don't want to go. Sometimes it can even take you completely out of the game. On the other hand, a good attitude puts you in the place of greatest potential.

Perhaps you're not sure if your attitude is where it ought to be. Or maybe you are leading someone whose attitude isn't as positive as it could be. How do you address that? First, you need to know how a person's attitude is formed. That's the subject of the next chapter.

PART II

THE FORMATION
OF ATTITUDE

3

WHAT SHAPES A PERSON'S ATTITUDE?

A lot goes into an attitude—but a lot more comes out of it!

Attitudes aren't shaped in a vacuum. People are born with certain characteristics, and those impact their attitudes. But many other factors play an even greater role in people's lives and in the formation of their attitudes. While these factors continually impact people, in general, they make the greatest impression during the following times of life:

STAGES	FACTORS
PRE-BIRTH:	Inherent personality/temperament
BIRTH:	Environment
AGES 1–6:	Word expression
	Adult acceptance/affirmation
AGES 6–10:	Self-image
	Exposure to new experiences
AGES 11–21:	Peers, physical appearance
AGES 21–61:	Marriage, family, job, success
	Adjustments, assessment of life

PERSONALITY—WHO I AM

All people are born as distinct individuals. Even two children with the same parents, same environment, and same training are totally different from each other. These differences contribute to the "spice of life" we all enjoy. Like tract homes that all look alike, if we all had similar personalities, our journey through life would certainly be boring.

GENERALLY, PEOPLE WITH CERTAIN TEMPERAMENTS DEVELOP SPECIFIC ATTITUDES COMMON TO THAT TEMPERAMENT.

I love the story of two men out fishing together who began discussing their wives. One said, "If all men were like me, they would all want to be married to my wife." The other man quickly replied, "If they were all like me, none of them would want to be married to her."

A set of attitudes accompanies each personality type. Generally, people with certain temperaments develop specific attitudes common to that temperament. A few years ago, Tim LaHaye, co-author of the popular "Left Behind" novels, lectured and wrote about the four basic temperaments. Through observation, I have noticed that a person with what he calls a *choleric* personality often exhibits attitudes of perseverance and aggressiveness. A *sanguine* person is generally positive and looks on the bright side of life. An introspective *melancholy* individual can be negative at times, while a *phlegmatic* is prone to say, "Easy come, easy go." Every individual's personality is composed of a mixture of these temperaments, and there are exceptions to these generalizations. However, a temperament ordinarily follows a track that can be identified by tracing a person's attitudes.

ENVIRONMENT—WHAT'S AROUND ME

I believe that environment is a greater controlling factor in our attitude development than our personality or other inherited traits. Before my wife, Margaret, and I began our family we decided to adopt our children. We wanted to give a child who might not normally have the benefit of a loving faith-filled home an opportunity to live in that environment. Although our children may not physically resemble us, they certainly have been molded by the environment in which we have reared them.

The environment of early childhood develops a person's "belief system." Children continually pick up priorities, attitudes, interests, and philosophies from their environment. It is a fact that what I really believe affects my attitude! However, the things I believe may not be true. What I believe may not be healthy. It may even hurt others and destroy me. Yet an attitude is reinforced by a belief—whether it is right or wrong.

Environment is the first influencer of our belief system. Therefore the foundation of an attitude is laid in the environment to which we were born. Environment becomes even more significant when we realize that the beginning attitudes are the most difficult to change.

WORD EXPRESSION—WHAT I HEAR

You've undoubtedly heard the old saying: "Sticks and stones may break my bones, but names will never hurt me." Don't you believe that! In fact, after the bruises have disappeared and the physical pain is gone, the inward pain of hurtful words remains.

Years ago when I was leading a church, during one of our staff meetings I asked the pastors, secretaries, and custodians to raise their hands if they could remember a childhood experience that hurt deeply because of someone's words. Everyone raised his hand. One pastor recalled the time when he sat in a reading circle at school. (Do you remember how intimidating those sessions were?) When his time came to read, he mispronounced the word *photography*. He read it photo-graphy instead of pho-tog-ra-phy. The teacher corrected him and the class laughed. He still remembers . . . forty years later. One positive result of that experience was his desire from that moment on to pronounce words correctly.

Today one of the reasons he excels as a speaker is be-cause of that determination.

Adult Acceptance/Affirmation— What I Feel

Often when I am speaking to leaders, I tell them about the importance of accepting and affirming the ones they are lead-ing. The truth is, people don't care how much you know until they know how much you care!

Think back to your school days. Who was your favorite teacher? Now think of why. Probably your warmest memo-ries are of someone who accepted and affirmed you. We sel-dom remember what our teacher said to us, but we do remember how they loved us. Long before we understand teaching, we reach out for understanding. Long after we have forgotten the teachings, we remember the feeling of acceptance or rejection.

PEOPLE DON'T CARE HOW MUCH YOU KNOW
UNTIL THEY KNOW HOW MUCH YOU CARE.

Many times I have asked people if they enjoyed their pas-tor's sermon the previous week. After a positive response I ask, "What was his subject?" Seventy-five percent of the time they cannot give me the sermon title. They do not remember the exact subject, but they do remember the atmosphere and attitude in which it was delivered.

My favorite Sunday school teachers from my childhood are beautiful examples of this truth. First came Katie, my second grade teacher. When I was sick and missed her class, she would come and visit me on Monday. She would ask how I was feeling and give me a five-cent trinket that was worth a million dollars to me. Katie would say, "Johnny, I always teach better when you are in the class. When you come next Sunday morning, would you raise your hand so I can see you are in attendance? Then I will teach better."

I can still remember raising my hand and watching Katie smile at me from the front of the class. I also remember other kids raising their hands on Sundays when Katie began to teach and her class grew rapidly. That year, the Sunday school superintendent wanted to split the class and start a new one across the hall. He asked for volunteers for the new class and no one raised his hand. Why? No kid wanted to go with a new teacher and miss Katie's continual demonstration of love.

Another teacher I remember is Glen Leatherwood. He taught all the junior high school boys in the church where I grew up. Did you ever teach a group of ten-wiggles-per-minute boys? Usually those teachers go straight from teaching that class to their heavenly reward! But not Glen. He taught junior high boys for another thirty years. The twelve months I spent in his class made a profound impact on my faith and my life's work.

I was also privileged to grow up in a very affirming family. I never questioned my parents' love and acceptance. They continually affirmed their love through actions and words. When our children were growing up, Margaret and I tried to create that same environment for them. I believe that our kids saw or sensed our acceptance and affirmation at least thirty times a day. Today I'd say our grandchildren get almost twice as much. That's not too much! Have you ever been told too many times that you are important, loved, and appreciated? Remember, people don't care how much you know until they know how much you care.

SELF-IMAGE—HOW I SEE MYSELF

It is impossible to perform consistently in a manner inconsistent with the way we see ourselves. In other words, we usually act in direct response to our self-image. Nothing is more difficult to accomplish than changing outward actions without changing inward feelings.

One of the best ways to improve those inward feelings is to put some "success" under your belt. My daughter Elizabeth has a tendency to be shy and wants to hold back on new experiences. But once she has warmed up to a situation, it's "full steam ahead." When she was in first grade, her school had a candy bar sale. Each child was given thirty candy bars and was challenged to sell every one of them. When I picked up Elizabeth from school she was holding her "challenge" and needed some positive encouragement. It was time for a sales meeting with my new salesgirl.

All the way home I taught her how to sell candy bars. I surrounded each teaching point with a half dozen "You can do it—your smile will win them over—I believe in you" phrases. By the end of our fifteen-minute drive, the young lady sitting beside me had become a charming, committed saleslady. Off she went to the neighborhood with little brother Joel eating one of the candy bars and declaring that it was truly the best he had ever devoured.

At the end of the day, all thirty bars had been sold and Elizabeth was feeling great. I will never forget the words she prayed as I tucked her into bed that night: "O God, thanks for the candy sale at school. It's great. O Lord, help make me a winner! Amen."

Elizabeth's prayer reflects the heart's desire of every person. We all want to be winners. Sure enough, Elizabeth came home the next day with another box of candy bars. Now the big test! She'd exhausted the supply of friendly neighbors, and she was thrust into the cruel world of the unknown buyer.

Elizabeth admitted fear as we went to a shopping center to sell our wares. Again I offered encouragement, a few more selling tips, more encouragement, the right location, more encouragement. And she did it. The experience amounted to two days of selling, two sold-out performances, two happy people, and one boosted self-image.

How we see ourselves reflects how others see us. If we like ourselves, it increases the odds that others will like us. Self-image sets the parameters for the construction of our attitudes. We act in response to how we see ourselves. We will never go beyond the boundaries that stake out our true feelings about ourselves. Those "new territories" can be explored only when our self-image is strong enough to give us permission to go there.

EXPOSURE TO NEW EXPERIENCES—
OPPORTUNITIES FOR GROWTH

French philosopher François Voltaire likened life to a game of cards. Each player must accept the cards dealt to him. But once those cards are in the hand, he alone decides how to play them to win the game.

We always have a number of opportunities in our hand, and we must decide whether to take a risk and act on them. Nothing in life causes more stress, yet at the same time provides more opportunity for growth, than new experiences.

If you are a parent, you will find it impossible to shield your children from new experiences that might be negative. So it is essential to prepare positive encounters that will build self-image and confidence. Both positive and negative experiences can be used as tools in preparing children for life.

Children need continual reassurance and praise when their new experiences are less than positive. In fact, the worse the experience, the more encouragement they need. But sometimes we become discouraged when they are discouraged. This is a good formula to adopt:

New experiences + teaching applications x love = growth.

ASSOCIATION WITH PEERS—
WHO INFLUENCES ME

What others indicate about their perceptions of us affects how we perceive ourselves. Usually we respond to the expectations of others. This truth becomes evident to parents when their children go to school. No longer can parents control their children's environment.

My parents understood that others could exercise a sizable amount of control over their sons' behavior, so they were determined to watch and control our peer relationships as much as possible. Their strategy: Provide a climate in the Maxwell home that was appealing to their two boys' friends. This meant sacrificing their finances and time. They provided us with a shuffleboard game, Ping-Pong table, pool table, pinball machine, chemistry set, basketball court, and all the sports equipment imaginable. We also had a mother who was spectator, referee, counselor, arbitrator, and fan.

And the kids came, often twenty to twenty-five at a time. All sizes, shapes, and colors. Everyone had fun and my parents observed our friends. Sometimes, after the gang had gone, my parents would ask about one of our friends. They would openly discuss his language or attitudes and encourage us not to act or think that way. I realize now that most of my major decisions as a young boy were influenced by my parents' teaching and observation of my associations.

Casey Stengel, who was a successful manager of the New York Yankees baseball team, understood the power of associations on a ballplayer's attitude. He gave Billy Martin some advice when he was a rookie manager. Martin recalled, "Casey said there would be fifteen players on your team who will run through a wall for you, five who will hate you, and five who are undecided. When you make out your rooming list, always room your losers together. Never room a good guy with a loser. Those losers who stay together will blame the manager for everything, but it won't spread if you keep them isolated."

Charles "Tremendous" Jones, author of *Life Is Tremendous*, says, "What you will become in five years will be determined by what you read and who you associate with." That's good for all of us to remember.

PHYSICAL APPEARANCE—
HOW WE LOOK TO OTHERS

Our looks play an important part in the construction of our attitude. Incredible pressure is placed upon people to possess the "in look," which seems to be the standard of acceptance. The next time you're watching television, notice how much the commercials emphasize looks. Notice the percentage of ads dealing with clothing, diet, exercise, and overall physical attractiveness. Hollywood says, "Blandness is out and beauty is in." This influences our perception of our worth.

What can make it even more difficult is the realization that others also judge our worth by our appearance. Recently, I read a business article that stated, "Our physical attractiveness helps determine our income." For example, the research reported in that article showed the discrepancies between the salaries of men 6'2" and 5'10". The taller men consistently received higher salaries. Like it or not, physical appearance (and one's perception of it) impacts a person's attitude.

Marriage, Family, and Job— Our Security and Status

New influences begin to affect our attitude as we approach our mid-twenties. It is during this time that most people start a career. They also often get married. That means another person influences our perspective.

When I speak on attitudes, I always emphasize the need to surround ourselves with positive people. One of the saddest comments that I often receive comes from someone who tells me their marriage partner is negative and doesn't want to change. To a certain extent, when the negative mate does not want to change, the positive one is imprisoned by negativism. In such situations I advise the couple to remember their spouse as the person they loved in their courtship days. Their marriage will improve if each other's weaknesses are not emphasized. But many end up in divorce court because the strengths are ignored. The partners go from expecting the best to expecting the worst, from building on strengths to focusing on weaknesses.

All of the factors I've mentioned go into the "mix" of attitude. They have impacted who you are and those whom you lead. But remember this: Whether you are eleven, forty-two, or sixty-five, your attitude toward life is *still* under construction. It's never too late for a person to change his attitude. And that's the subject of the next chapter.

4

CAN AN ATTITUDE BE CHANGED?

The key to having a good attitude
is the willingness to change.

We are either the masters or the victims of our attitudes. It is a matter of personal choice. Who we are today is the result of choices we made yesterday. Tomorrow we will become what we choose today. To change means to choose to change.

I'm told that in northern Canada there are just two seasons: winter and July. When the back roads begin to thaw, they become muddy. Vehicles going into the backwoods country leave deep ruts that become frozen when cold weather returns. For those entering remote areas during the winter months, there are signs that read, "Driver, please choose carefully which rut you drive in, because you'll be in it for the next twenty miles."

Some people seem to feel stuck in their current attitudes, like a car in a twenty-mile rut. However, attitude is not permanent. If you're not happy with yours, know that you can change it. If someone you lead has a bad attitude, then you can help them to change—but only if they truly *want* to change. Anyone can become the kind of positive person for whom life is a joy and every day is filled with potential if they genuinely desire to.

If you want to have a great attitude, then make the following choices:

CHOICE #1: EVALUATE YOUR PRESENT ATTITUDE

The process begins with knowing where you're starting from. Evaluating your present attitude will take some time. If possible, try to separate yourself from your attitude. The goal of this exercise is not to see the "bad you" but a "bad attitude" that keeps you from being a more fulfilled person. You can make key changes only when you identify the problem.

When he sees a logjam, the professional logger climbs a tall tree and locates a key log, blows that log free, and lets the stream do the rest. An amateur would start at the edge of the jam and move all the logs, eventually moving the key log. Obviously, both methods will get the logs moving, but the professional does his work more quickly and effectively.

To find the key "logs" in your attitude, use the following evaluation process (and write your answers in a journal or someplace where you can later refer back to them):

Identify Problem Feelings: What attitudes make you feel the most negative about yourself? Usually feelings can be sensed before the problem is clarified.

Identify Problem Behavior: What attitudes cause you the most problems when dealing with others?

Identify Problem Thinking: We are the sum of our thoughts. "As a man thinks within himself, so he is."[1] What thoughts consistently control your mind? Although this is the beginning step in correcting attitude problems, these are not as easy to identify as the first two.

Clarify Truth: In order to know how to change, you need to examine your feelings in light of truth. If you are a person of faith, then use the Scriptures. What do they tell you about how your attitude should be?

Secure Commitment: At this stage, "What must I do to change?" turns into "I must change." Remember, the choice to change is the one decision that must be made, and only you can make it.

Plan and Carry Out Your Choice: Act on your decision immediately and repeatedly.

CHOICE #2: REALIZE THAT FAITH IS STRONGER THAN FEAR

The only thing that will guarantee the success of a difficult or doubtful undertaking is faith from the beginning that you can do it. Philosopher William James said, "The greatest discovery of my generation is that people can alter their lives by altering their attitudes of mind." Change depends on your frame of mind. Believe that you can change. Ask your friends and colleagues to encourage you at every opportunity. And if you are a person of faith, ask for God's help. He knows your problems, and He is willing and able to help you overcome them.

CHOICE #3: WRITE A STATEMENT OF PURPOSE

When I was a boy, my father decided to build a basketball court for my brother and me. He made a cement driveway, put a backboard on the garage and was just getting ready to put up the basket when he was called away on an emergency. He promised to put up the hoop as soon as he returned. *No problem,* I thought. *I have a brand-new Spalding ball and a new cement driveway on which to dribble it.* For a few minutes I bounced the ball on the cement. Soon that became boring, so I took the ball and threw it up against the backboard—once. I let the ball run off the court and didn't pick it up again until Dad returned to put up the rim. Why? It's no fun playing basketball without a goal. The joy is in having something to aim for.

In order to have fun and direction in changing your attitude, you must establish a clearly stated goal. This goal should be as specific as possible, written out and signed, with a time frame attached to it. The purpose statement should be placed in a visible spot where you see it several times a day to give you reinforcement.

You will attain this goal if each day you do three things:

1. Write specifically what you desire to accomplish each day.

The biblical story of David's encounter with Goliath is a fine illustration of faith and how it may overcome insurmountable odds with seemingly inadequate resources. But one thing perplexed me when I first began to study David's life. Why did he pick five stones for his sling on his way to encounter Goliath? The longer I pondered, the more perplexed I became. Why five stones? There was only one giant. Choosing five stones seemed to be a flaw in his faith. Did he think he was going to miss and that he would have four more chances? Some time later I was reading in 2 Samuel, and I got the answer. Goliath had four sons, so that means there were five giants. In David's reckoning, there was one stone per giant! Now that is what I mean about being specific in our faith.

What are the giants you must slay to make your attitude what it needs to be? What resources will you need? Don't be overcome with frustration when you see the problems. Take one giant at a time. Military strategists teach their armies to fight one front at a time. Settle which attitude you want to tackle at this time. Write it down. As you successfully begin to win battles, write them down. And spend time reading about past victories because it will encourage you.

2. VERBALIZE TO AN ENCOURAGING FRIEND WHAT YOU WANT TO ACCOMPLISH EACH DAY.

Belief is inward conviction; faith is outward action. You will receive both encouragement and accountability by verbalizing your intentions. One of the ways people resolve a conflict is to verbalize it to themselves or someone else. This practice is also vital in reaching your desired attitudes.

I know successful salesmen who repeat this phrase out loud fifty times each morning and fifty times each evening: "I can do it." Continually saying positive statements helps them believe in themselves and causes them to act on that belief. Start this process by changing your vocabulary. Here are some suggestions:

ELIMINATE THESE WORDS COMPLETELY	MAKE THESE WORDS A PART OF YOUR VOCABULARY
1. I can't	1. I can
2. If	2. I will

3. Doubt	3. Expect the best
4. I don't think	4. I know
5. I don't have the time	5. I will make the time
6. Maybe	6. Positively
7. I'm afraid of	7. I am confident
8. I don't believe	8. I do believe
9. (minimize) I	9. (promote) You
10. It's impossible	10. All things are possible

3. TAKE ACTION ON YOUR GOAL EACH DAY.

The difference between a wise man and a foolish one is his response to what he already knows: A wise man follows up on what he hears while a foolish man knows but does not act. To change, you must take action. And while you're at it, do something positive for someone else too. Nothing improves a person's outlook like unselfish service to someone with a greater need than their own.

CHOICE #4: HAVE THE DESIRE TO CHANGE

No choice will determine the success of your attitude change more than desiring to change. When all else fails, desire alone can keep you heading in the right direction. Many people have climbed over insurmountable obstacles to make themselves better when they realized that change is possible if they want it badly enough. Let me illustrate.

While hopping about one day, a frog happened to slip into a very large pothole along a country road. All of his attempts at jumping out were in vain. Soon a rabbit came upon the frog trapped in the hole and offered to help him out. He, too, failed. After various animals from the forest made three or four gallant attempts to help the poor frog out, they finally gave up. "We'll go back and get you some food," they said. "It looks like you're going to be here a while." However, not long after they took off to get food, they heard the frog hopping along after them. They couldn't believe it! "We thought you couldn't get out!" they exclaimed. "Oh, I couldn't," replied the frog. "But you see, there was a big truck coming right at me, and I had to."

FALL IN LOVE WITH THE CHALLENGE OF CHANGE AND WATCH THE DESIRE TO CHANGE GROW.

It is when we "have to get out of the potholes of life" that we change. As long as we have acceptable options, we will not change. The truth is that most people are more comfortable with old problems than new solutions. They respond to their needs for a turnaround in life like the Duke of Cambridge, who once said, "Any change, at any time, for any reason, is to be deplored." People who believe that nothing should ever be done for the first time never see anything done.

People can change, and that is the greatest motivation of all. Nothing sparks the fires of desire more than the sudden realization that you do not have to stay the same. Fall in love with the challenge of change and watch the desire to change grow. That's what happened to Aleida Huissen, seventy-eight, of Rotterdam, Netherlands. She had been a smoker for fifty years, and for fifty years she tried to give up the habit. But she was unsuccessful. Then Leo Jensen, seventy-nine, proposed marriage and refused to go through with the wedding until Aleida gave up smoking. Aleida says, "Willpower never was enough to get me off the habit. Love did it."

My life is dedicated to helping others reach their potential. I suggest that you follow the advice of Mark Twain, who said, "Take your mind out every now and then and dance on it. It is getting all caked up." It was his way of saying, "Get out of that rut." Too many times we settle into a set way of thinking and accept limitations that need not be placed upon us. Embrace change, and it will change you.

Choice #5: Live One Day at a Time

Any person can fight the battle for just one day. It is only when you and I add the burdens of those two awful eternities, yesterday and tomorrow, that we tremble. It is not the experiences of today that drive people to distraction; it is the remorse or bitterness for something that happened yesterday and the dread of what tomorrow may bring. Let us therefore live but one day at a time—today!

Choice #6: Change Your Thought Patterns

That which holds our attention determines our actions. We are where we are and what we are because of the dominating thoughts that occupy our minds. Take a look at this syllogism. It emphasizes the power of our thought life:

Major premise: We can control our thoughts.
Minor premise: Our feelings come from our thoughts.
Conclusion: We can control our feelings by learning to change how we think.

It is that simple. Our feelings come from our thoughts. Therefore, we can change them by changing our thought patterns.

Our thought life, not our circumstances, determines our happiness. Often I see people who are convinced that they will be happy when they attain a certain goal. When they reach the goal, many times they do not find the fulfillment they anticipated. The secret to staying on an even keel? Fill your mind with good thoughts. The apostle Paul advised, "Whatever things are true, whatever things are noble . . . whatever things are of good report, if there is any virtue and if there is anything praiseworthy—meditate on these things."[2] He understood that the things that hold our attention determine our action.

Choice #7: Develop Good Habits

An attitude is nothing more than a habit of thought. The process for developing habits—good or bad—is the same. It is as easy to form the habit of succeeding as it is to succumb to the habit of failure.

Habits aren't instincts; they're acquired actions or reactions. They don't just happen; they are caused. Once the original cause of a habit is determined, it is within your power to accept or reject it. Most people allow their habits to control them. When those habits are hurtful, they negatively impact their attitudes.

The following steps will assist you in changing bad habits into good ones:

Step #1: List your bad habits.
Step #2: What was the original cause?

Step #3:   What are the supporting causes?

Step #4:   Determine a positive habit to replace the bad one.

Step #5:   Think about the good habit, its benefits and results.

Step #6:   Take action to develop this habit.

Step #7:   Daily act upon this habit for reinforcement.

Step #8:   Reward yourself by noting one of the benefits from your good habit.

CHOICE #8—CONTINUALLY CHOOSE TO HAVE A RIGHT ATTITUDE

Once you make the choice to possess a good attitude, the work has only just begun. After that comes a life of continually deciding to grow and maintaining the right outlook. Attitudes have a tendency to revert back to their original patterns if they are not carefully guarded and cultivated.

As you work to improve your attitude or to help the attitude of someone you lead, recognize that there are three stages of change where a person must deliberately choose the right attitude:

Early Stage: The first few days are always the most difficult. Old habits are hard to break. You must continually be on guard mentally to take the right action.

Middle Stage: The moment good habits begin to take root,

options open that bring on new challenges. During this stage, new habits will form that can be good or bad. The good news is that the more right choices and habits you develop, the more likely other good habits will be formed.

Later Stage: In the later stage, complacency is the enemy. We all know someone (perhaps us) who lost weight only to fall back into old eating habits and gain it back. Don't let down your guard until the change is complete. And even then, be vigilant and make sure you don't fall into old negative habits.

You are the only one who can determine what you will think and how you will act. And that means you can make your attitude what you want it to be. But even if you succeed and become a positive person, that won't shield you from negative experiences. How does a positive person deal with obstacles and remain upbeat? To find the answer to that question, read the next chapter.

5

CAN OBSTACLES ACTUALLY
ENHANCE AN ATTITUDE?

*The greatest battle you wage against failure occurs
on the inside, not the outside.*

Working artists David Bayles and Ted Orland tell a story about an art teacher who did an experiment with his grading system for two groups of students. It is a parable on the benefits of failure. Here is what happened:

The ceramics teacher announced on opening day that he was dividing the class into two groups. All those on the left side of the studio, he said, would be graded solely on the quantity of work they produced, all those on the right solely on its quality. His procedure was simple: on the final day of class he would bring in his bathroom scale and weigh the work of the "quantity" group: fifty pounds of pots rated an "A," forty pounds a "B," and so on. Those being graded on "quality," however, needed to produce only one pot—albeit a perfect one—to get an "A." Well, come grading time and a curious fact emerged:

the works of the highest quality were all produced by the group being graded for quantity. It seems that while the "quantity" group was busily churning out piles of work—and learning from their mistakes—the "quality" group had sat theorizing about perfection, and in the end had little more to show for their efforts than grandiose theories and a pile of dead clay.[1]

It doesn't matter whether your objectives are in the area of art, business, ministry, sports, or relationships. The only way you can get ahead is to fail early, fail often, and fail forward.

Take the Journey

I teach leadership to thousands of people each year at numerous conferences. And one of my greatest concerns is always that some people will go home from the event and nothing will change in their lives. They enjoy the "show" but fail to implement any of the ideas that were presented to them. I tell people continually: We overestimate the event and underestimate the process. Every dream that anyone has achieved came because of dedication to a process. (That's one of the reasons I write books and create audio programs—so that people can engage in the ongoing process of growth.)

People naturally tend toward inertia. That's why self-improvement is such a struggle. But that's also the reason that adversity lies at the heart of every success. The process of achievement comes through repeated failures and the constant struggle to climb to a higher level.

IN ORDER TO ACHIEVE YOUR DREAMS,
YOU MUST EMBRACE ADVERSITY AND MAKE FAILURE A
REGULAR PART OF YOUR LIFE. IF YOU'RE NOT FAILING,
YOU'RE PROBABLY NOT REALLY MOVING FORWARD.

When it comes to facing failure, most people will grudgingly concede that any person must make it through some adversity in order to succeed. They'll acknowledge that you have to experience the occasional setback to make progress. But I believe that success comes only if you take that thought one step further. In order to achieve your dreams, you must embrace adversity and make failure a regular part of your life. If you're not failing, you're probably not really moving forward.

THE BENEFITS OF ADVERSITY

Psychologist Dr. Joyce Brothers asserts, "The person interested in success has to learn to view failure as a healthy, inevitable part of the process of getting to the top." Adversity and the failure that often results from it should not only be expected in the process of succeeding; they need to be viewed as an absolutely critical part of it. In fact, the benefits of adversity are many. Take a look at some of the key reasons to embrace adversity and persevere through it:

1. Adversity Creates Resilience

Nothing in life breeds resilience like adversity and failure. A study in *Time* magazine in the mid-1980s described the incredible resilience of a group of people who had lost their jobs three times because of plant closings. Psychologists expected them to be discouraged, but they were surprisingly optimistic. Their adversity had actually created an advantage. Because they had already lost a job and found a new one at least twice, they were better able to handle adversity than people who had worked for only one company and found themselves unemployed.[2]

2. Adversity Develops Maturity

Adversity can make you better if you don't let it make you bitter. Why? Because it promotes wisdom and maturity. American novelist William Saroyan said, "Good people are good because they've come to wisdom through failure. We get very little wisdom from success, you know."

As the world continues to change at a faster and faster rate, maturity with flexibility becomes increasingly important. Those qualities come from weathering difficulties. Harvard business school professor John Kotter says, "I can imagine a group of executives 20 years ago discussing a candidate for a top job and saying, 'This guy had a big failure when he was 32.' Everyone else would say, 'Yep, yep, that's a bad sign.' I can imagine that same group considering a candidate today and saying, 'What worries me about this guy is that he's never failed.'"[3] The problems we face and overcome prepare us for future difficulties.

3. ADVERSITY PUSHES THE ENVELOPE OF ACCEPTED PERFORMANCE

Lloyd Ogilvie says that a friend of his, who was a circus performer in his youth, described his experience of learning to work on the trapeze as follows:

> Once you know that the net below will catch you, you stop worrying about falling. You actually learn to fall successfully! What that means is, you can concentrate on catching the trapeze swinging toward you, and not on falling, because repeated falls in the past have convinced you that the net is strong and reliable when you do fall . . . The result of falling and being caught by the net is a mysterious confidence and daring on the trapeze. You fall less. Each fall makes you able to risk more.[4]

Until a person learns from personal experience that he can live through adversity, he is reluctant to buck mindless tradition, push the envelope of organizational performance, or challenge himself to press his physical limits. Failure helps prompt people to rethink the status quo.

4. ADVERSITY PROVIDES GREATER OPPORTUNITIES

I believe that eliminating problems limits our potential. Just about every successful entrepreneur I've met has numerous stories of adversity and setbacks that opened doors to greater opportunity. For example, in 1978 Bernie Marcus, the son of a poor Russian cabinetmaker in Newark, New Jersey, was fired from Handy Dan, a do-it-yourself hardware retailer. That prompted Marcus to team with Arthur Blank to start their own business. In 1979, they opened their first store in Atlanta, Georgia. It was called Home Depot. Today, Home Depot has more than 760 stores employing more than 157,000 people; they have expanded the business to include overseas operations; and each year they do more than $30 billion in sales.

I'm sure Bernie Marcus wasn't very happy about getting fired from his job back at Handy Dan. But if he hadn't been, who knows whether he would have achieved the success he has today.

5. ADVERSITY PROMPTS INNOVATION

Early in the twentieth century, a boy whose family had emigrated from Sweden to Illinois sent twenty-five cents to a publisher for a book on photography. What he received instead was a book on ventriloquism. What did he do? He adapted and learned ventriloquism. He was Edgar Bergen, and for over forty years he entertained audiences with the help of a wooden dummy named Charlie McCarthy.

The ability to innovate is at the heart of creativity—a vital component in success. University of Houston professor Jack Matson recognized that fact and developed a course that his students call "Failure 101." In it, Matson has students build mock-ups of products that no one would ever buy. His goal is to get students to equate failure with innovation instead of defeat. That way they will free themselves to try new things. "They learn to reload and get ready to shoot again," says Matson. If you want to succeed, you have to learn to make adjustments to the way you do things and try again. Adversity helps to develop that ability.

6. ADVERSITY BRINGS UNEXPECTED BENEFITS

The average person makes a mistake, and automatically thinks that it's a failure. But some of the greatest stories of success can be found in the unexpected benefits of mistakes. For example, most people are familiar with the story of Edison and the phonograph: He discovered it while trying to invent something entirely different. But did you also know that Kellogg's Corn Flakes resulted when boiled wheat was left in a baking pan overnight? Or that Ivory soap floats because a batch was left in the mixer too long and had a large volume of air whipped into it? Or that Scott Towels were launched when a toilet paper machine put too many layers of tissue together?

"IN SCIENCE, MISTAKES ALWAYS PRECEDE THE TRUTH."
—HORACE WALPOLE

Horace Walpole said that "in science, mistakes always precede the truth." That's what happened to German-Swiss chemist Christian Friedrich Schönbein. One day he was working in the kitchen—which his wife had strictly forbidden—and was experimenting with sulfuric and nitric acid. When he accidentally spilled some of the mixture on the kitchen table, he thought he was in trouble. (He knew he would experience "adversity" when his wife found out!) He hurriedly snatched up a cotton apron, wiped up the mess, and hung the apron by the fire to dry.

Suddenly there was a violent explosion. Evidently the cellulose in the cotton underwent a process called "nitration." Unwittingly, Schönbein had invented nitrocellulose—what came to be called smokeless gunpowder or gun-cotton. He went on to market his invention, which made him a lot of money.

7. ADVERSITY MOTIVATES

Years ago when Bear Bryant was coaching the University of Alabama's football team, the Crimson Tide was ahead by only six points in a game with less than two minutes remaining in the fourth quarter. Bryant sent his quarterback into the game with instructions to play it safe and run out the clock.

In the huddle, the quarterback said, "Coach says to play it safe, but that's what they're expecting. Let's give them a surprise." And with that, he called a pass play.

When the quarterback dropped back and threw the pass, the defending cornerback, who was a champion sprinter, intercepted the ball and headed for the end zone expecting to score a touchdown. The quarterback, who was not known as a good runner, took off after the cornerback and ran him down from behind, tackling him on the five-yard line. It saved the game.

After the clock ran out, the opposing coach approached Bear Bryant and said, "What's this business about your quarterback not being a runner? He ran down my speedster from behind!"

Bryant responded, "Your man was running for six points. My man was running for his life."

Nothing can motivate a person like adversity. Olympic diver Pat McCormick said, "I think failure is one of the great motivators. After my narrow loss in the 1948 trials, I knew how really good I could be. It was the defeat that focused all my concentration on my training and goals." McCormick went on to win two gold medals in the Olympics in London that year and another two in Helsinki four years later.

If you can step back from the negative circumstances you face in life, you will be able to discover that there are positive benefits to your negative experiences. That is almost always true; you simply have to be willing to look for them—and not take the adversity you are experiencing too personally.

So if you lose your job, think about the resilience you're developing. If you try something daring and survive, think about what you learned about yourself—and how it will help you take on new challenges. If a restaurant gets your order wrong, figure out if it's an opportunity to learn a new skill. And if you experience a train wreck in your career, think of the maturity it's developing in you. Besides, Bill Vaughan says, "In the game of life it's a good idea to have a few early losses, which relieves you of the pressure of trying to maintain an undefeated season." Always measure an obstacle next to the size of the dream you're pursuing. It's all in how you look at it. Try, and you can find the good in every bad experience.

WHAT COULD BE WORSE?

One of the most incredible stories of adversity overcome and success gained is that of Joseph of the ancient Hebrews. You may be familiar with the story. He was born the eleventh of twelve sons in a wealthy Middle Eastern family whose trade was raising livestock. As a teenager, Joseph alienated his brothers: First, he was his father's favorite, even though he was nearly the youngest. Second, he used to tell his father any time his brothers weren't doing their work properly with the sheep. And third, he made the mistake of telling his older brothers that one day he would be in charge of them. At first a group of his brothers wanted to kill him, but the eldest, Reuben, prevented them from doing that. So when Reuben wasn't around, the others sold him into slavery.

Joseph ended up in Egypt working in the house of the captain of the guard, a man named Potiphar. Because of his leadership and administrative skill, Joseph quickly rose in the ranks, and before long, he was running the entire household. He was making the best of a bad situation. But then things got worse. The wife of his master tried to persuade him to sleep with her. When he refused, she accused him of making advances toward her, and got Potiphar to throw Joseph in prison.

From Slavery to Prison

At that point Joseph was in about as difficult a position as he could be. He was separated from his family. He was living away from home in a foreign land. He was a slave. And he was in prison. But again, he made the best of a tough situation. Before long, the warden of the prison put Joseph in charge of all the prisoners and all the prison's daily activities.

While in prison, Joseph got the chance to meet a fellow prisoner who had been an official from Pharaoh's court, the chief cupbearer. And Joseph was able to do him a favor by interpreting a dream the man had. When he saw that the official was grateful, Joseph made a request of him in return.

"When all goes well with you," Joseph asked, "remember me and show me kindness; mention me to Pharaoh and get me out of this prison. For I was forcibly carried off from the land of the Hebrews, and even here I have done nothing to deserve being put in a dungeon."[5]

Joseph had great hope a few days later when the official was returned to court and the good graces of the monarch. He expected any minute to receive word that Pharaoh was setting him free. But he waited. And waited. Two years passed before the cupbearer remembered Joseph, and he did so only because Pharaoh wanted someone to interpret one of his dreams.

FINALLY . . . THE PAYOFF

In the end, Joseph was able to interpret Pharaoh's dreams. And because the Hebrew showed such great wisdom, the Egyptian ruler put Joseph in charge of the entire kingdom. As the result of Joseph's leadership, planning, and system of food storage, when famine struck the Middle East seven years later, many thousands of people who otherwise would have died were able to survive—including Joseph's own family. When his brothers traveled to Egypt for relief from the famine—twenty years after selling him into slavery—they discovered that their brother Joseph was not only alive, but second in command of the most powerful kingdom in the world.

Few people would welcome the adversity of thirteen years in bondage as a slave and prisoner. But as far as we know, Joseph never gave up hope and never lost his perspective. Nor did he hold a grudge against his brothers. After their father died, he told them, "You intended to harm me, but God intended it for good to accomplish what is now being done, the saving of many lives."

Joseph found the positive benefits in his negative experiences. And if he can do it, so can we. To help you do that, you need to take the next step when it comes to attitude. You have to be able to deal positively with failure.

PART III

THE FUTURE WITH THE RIGHT ATTITUDE

6

WHAT IS FAILURE?

*Every successful person is someone who failed,
yet never regarded himself as a failure.*

In an interview years ago David Brinkley asked advice columnist Ann Landers what question she most frequently received from readers. Her answer: "What's wrong with me?"

Landers's response reveals a lot about human nature. Many people wrestle with feelings of failure, the most damaging being doubtful thoughts about themselves. At the heart of those doubts and feelings is one central question: Am I a failure? And that's a problem because I believe it's nearly impossible for any person to believe he is a failure and succeed at the same time. Instead, you have to meet failure with the right attitude and determine to fail forward.

It seems that advice columnists (such as the late Ann Landers) and humor writers recognize that keeping a good attitude about yourself is important to overcoming adversity and mistakes. The late Erma Bombeck, who wrote a widely syndicated weekly humor column until a few weeks before her death in 1996, had a firm grasp on what it meant to persevere and fail forward without taking failure too personally.

From Newspaper Copy Girl to *Time* Magazine Cover Girl

Erma Bombeck traveled a road that was filled with adversity, starting with her career. She was drawn to journalism early in life. Her first job was as a copy girl at the *Dayton Journal-Herald* when she was a teenager. But when she went off to college at Ohio University, a guidance counselor advised her, "Forget about writing." She refused. Later she transferred to the University of Dayton and in 1949 graduated with a degree in English. Soon afterward she began working as a writer—for the obituary column and the women's page.

That year adversity carried over into her personal life. When she got married, one of her deepest desires was to become a mother. But much to her dismay, her doctors told her she was incapable of having children. Did she give up and consider herself a failure? No, she and her husband explored the possibility of adoption, and then they adopted a daughter.

Two years later, a surprised Erma became pregnant. But even that brought her more difficulties. In four years she experienced four pregnancies, but only two of the babies survived.

In 1964 Erma was able to convince the editor of a small neighborhood newspaper, the *Kettering-Oakwood Times*, to let her write a weekly humor column. Despite the pitiful $3 per article she was paid, she kept writing. And that opened a door for her. The next year she was offered the opportunity to write a three-times-a-week column for her old employer, the *Dayton Journal-Herald*. By 1967 her column was syndicated and carried by more than nine hundred newspapers.

For slightly more than thirty years Erma wrote her humor column. During that time she published fifteen books, was recognized as one of the twenty-five most influential women in America, appeared frequently on the television show *Good Morning America*, was featured on the cover of *Time* magazine, received innumerable honors (such as the American Cancer Society's Medal of Honor), and was awarded fifteen honorary degrees.

More Than Her Share of Problems

But during that span of time, Erma Bombeck also experienced incredible troubles and trials, including breast cancer, a mastectomy, and kidney failure. And she wasn't shy about sharing her perspective on her life experiences:

I speak at college commencements, and I tell everyone I'm up there and they're down there, not because of my successes, but my failures. Then I proceed to spin all of them off—a comedy record album that sold two copies in Beirut . . . a sit-com that lasted about as long as a donut in our house . . . a Broadway play that never saw Broadway . . . book signings where I attracted two people: one who wanted directions to the restroom and the other who wanted to buy the desk.

What you have to tell yourself is, "I'm not a failure. I failed at doing something." There's a big difference . . . Personally and career-wise, it's been a corduroy road. I've buried babies, lost parents, had cancer, and worried over kids. The trick is to put it all in perspective . . . and that's what I do for a living.[1]

That winning attitude kept Erma Bombeck down to earth. (She liked to refer to herself as "a former homeroom mother and obituary writer.") It also kept her going—and writing—through the disappointments, the pain, the surgeries, and the daily kidney dialysis until her death at age sixty-nine.

EVERY GENIUS COULD HAVE BEEN A "FAILURE"

Every successful person is someone who failed, yet never regarded himself as a failure. For example, Wolfgang Mozart, one of the geniuses of musical composition, was told by Emperor Ferdinand that his opera *The Marriage of Figaro* was "far too noisy" and contained "far too many notes." Artist Vincent van Gogh, whose paintings now set records for the sums they bring at auction, sold only one painting in his lifetime. Thomas Edison, the most prolific inventor in history, was considered unteachable as a youngster. And Albert Einstein, the greatest thinker of our time, was told by a Munich schoolmaster that he would "never amount to much."

I think it's safe to say that all great achievers are given multiple reasons to believe they are failures. But in spite of that, they remain positive and they persevere. In the face of adversity, rejection, and failings, they continue believing in themselves and refuse to consider themselves failures. They chose to develop the right attitude about failure.

FAILING FORWARD IS NOT FALSE SELF-ESTEEM

I place high value on praising people, especially children. In fact, I believe that people live up to your level of expectation. But I also believe that you have to base your praise on truth. You don't make up nice things to say about others. Here's the approach I use to encourage and lead others:

Value people.

Praise effort.

Reward performance.

I use that method with everyone. I even use a form of it with myself. When I'm working, I don't give myself a reward until after the job is finished. When I approach a task or project, I give it my very best, and no matter what the results are, I have a clear conscience. I have no problem sleeping at night. And no matter where I fail or how many mistakes I make, I don't let it devalue my worth as a person. As the saying goes, "God uses people who fail—'cause there aren't any other kind around."

It is possible to cultivate a positive attitude about yourself, no matter what circumstances you find yourself in or what kind of history you have.

SEVEN ABILITIES NEEDED TO FAIL FORWARD

Here are seven abilities of achievers that enable them to fail, not take it personally, and keep moving forward:

1. REJECT REJECTION

Author James Allen states, "A man is literally what he thinks, his character being the complete sum of all his thought." That's why it's important to make sure your thinking is on the right track.

People who don't give up keep trying because they don't base their self-worth on their performance. Instead, they have an internally based self-image. Rather than say, "I am a failure," they say, "I missed that one," or "I made a mistake."

Psychologist Martin E. Seligman believes we have two choices when we fail: We can internalize or externalize our failure. "People who blame themselves when they fail . . . think they are worthless, talentless, unlovable," says Seligman. "People who blame external events do not lose self-esteem when bad events strike."[2] To keep the right perspective, take responsibility for your actions, but don't take failure personally.

2. SEE FAILURE AS TEMPORARY

People who personalize failure see a problem as a hole they're permanently stuck in. But achievers see any predicament as temporary. For example, take the case of United States President Harry S. Truman. In 1922 he was thirty-eight years old, in debt, and out of work. In 1945 he was the most powerful leader of the free world, occupying the highest office in the land. If he had seen failure as permanent, he would have remained stuck and never would have kept trying and believing in his potential.

3. SEE FAILURES AS ISOLATED INCIDENTS

Author Leo Buscaglia once talked about his admiration for cooking expert Julia Child: "I just love her attitude. She says, 'Tonight we're going to make a soufflé!' And she beats this and whisks that, and she drops things on the floor . . . and does all these wonderful human things. Then she takes the soufflé and throws it in the oven and talks to you for a while. Finally, she says, 'Now it's ready!' But when she opens the oven, the soufflé just falls flat as a pancake. But does she panic or burst into tears? No! She smiles and says, 'Well, you can't win them all. Bon appetit!'"

When achievers fail, they see it as a momentary event, not a lifelong epidemic. It's not personal. If you want to succeed, don't let any single incident color your view of yourself.

4. KEEP EXPECTATIONS REALISTIC

The greater the feat you desire to achieve, the greater the mental preparation required for overcoming obstacles and persevering over the long haul. If you want to take a stroll in your neighborhood, you can reasonably expect to have few, if any, problems. But that's not the case if you intend to climb Mount Everest.

It takes time, effort, and the ability to overcome setbacks. You have to approach each day with reasonable expectations and not get your feelings hurt when everything doesn't turn out perfectly.

Something that happened on baseball's opening day in 1954 illustrates the point well. The Milwaukee Braves and the Cincinnati Reds played each other, and a rookie for each team made his major-league debut during that game. The rookie who played for the Reds hit four doubles and helped his team win with a score of 9-8. The rookie for the Braves went 0 for 5. The Reds player was Jim Greengrass, a name you probably haven't heard. The other guy, who didn't get a hit, might be more familiar to you. His name was Hank Aaron, the player who became the best home-run hitter in the history of baseball.

If Aaron's expectations for that first game had been unrealistic, who knows? He might have given up baseball. Surely he wasn't happy about his performance that day, but he didn't think of himself as a failure. He had worked too hard for too long. He wasn't about to give up easily.

5. FOCUS ON STRENGTHS

Another way achievers keep themselves from personalizing failure is by focusing on their strengths. Bob Butera, former president of the New Jersey Devils hockey team, was asked what makes a winner. He answered, "What distinguishes winners from losers is that winners concentrate at all times on what they can do, not on what they can't do. If a guy is a great shooter but not a great skater, we tell him to think only about the shot, the shot, the shot—never about some other guy outskating him. The idea is to remember your successes."

If a weakness is a matter of character, it needs much attention. Focus on it until you shore it up. Otherwise, the best bet for failing forward is developing and maximizing your strengths.

6. VARY APPROACHES TO ACHIEVEMENT

In *The Psychology of Achievement*, Brian Tracy writes about four millionaires who made their fortunes by age thirty-five. They were involved in an average of seventeen businesses before finding the one that took them to the top. They kept trying and changing until they found something that worked for them.

Achievers are willing to vary their approaches to problems. That's important in every walk of life, not just business. For example, if you're a fan of track-and-field events, you have undoubtedly enjoyed watching athletes compete in the high jump. I'm always amazed by the heights achieved by the men and women in that event. What's really interesting is that in the 1960s, the sport went through a major change in technique that allowed athletes to break the old records and push them up to new levels.

The person responsible for that change was Dick Fosbury. Where previous athletes used the straddle method to high jump, in which they went over the bar while facing it, with one arm and one leg leading, Fosbury developed a technique where he went over headfirst with his back to the bar. It was dubbed the Fosbury Flop.

Developing a new high-jump technique was one thing. Getting it accepted by others was another matter. Fosbury remarked, "I was told over and over again that I would never be successful, that I was not going to be competitive and the technique was simply not going to work. All I could do was shrug and say, 'We'll just have to see.'"

And people did see. Fosbury won the gold medal in the Mexico City Olympics in 1968, shattering the previous Olympic record and setting a new world record in the process. Since then, nearly all world-class high jumpers have used his technique. To achieve his goals, Fosbury varied his approach to high jumping, and he kept a positive attitude by not allowing others' comments to make him feel like a failure.

7. BOUNCE BACK

All achievers have in common the ability to bounce back after an error, mistake, or failure. Psychologist Simone

Caruthers says, "Life is a series of outcomes. Sometimes the outcome is what you want. Great. Figure out what you did right. Sometimes the outcome is what you don't want. Great. Figure out what you did so you don't do it again."[3] The key to bouncing back is found in your attitude toward the outcome.

Achievers are able to keep moving forward no matter what happens. And that's made possible because they remember that failure does not make *them* failures. No one should take mistakes personally. That's the best way to pick yourself up after failure and continue with a positive attitude. Once you do that, you're ready for success, which happens to be the subject of the next chapter.

7

WHAT IS SUCCESS?

*Attitude determines how far you can go
on the success journey.*

Do you want to be successful? The problem for most people who want to be successful is *not* that they can't achieve success. The main obstacle for them is that they misunderstand success. They don't have the right *attitude* about it. Maltbie D. Babcock said, "One of the most common mistakes and one of the costliest is thinking that success is due to some genius, some magic, something or other which we do not possess."

What is success? What does it look like? Most people have a vague picture of what it means to be a successful person that looks something like this:

The wealth of Bill Gates,
the physique of Arnold Schwarzenegger,
(or Tyra Banks),
the intelligence of Albert Einstein,

the athletic ability of Michael Jordan,
the business prowess of Donald Trump,
the social grace and poise of Jackie Kennedy,
the imagination of Walt Disney, and
the heart of Mother Teresa.

That sounds absurd, but it's closer to the truth than we would like to admit. Many of us picture success as looking like someone other than who we are. That's the wrong way to think about it. If you tried to become just like even one of these other people, you wouldn't be successful. You would be a bad imitation of them, and you would eliminate the possibility of becoming the person you were meant to be.

THE WRONG ATTITUDE ABOUT SUCCESS

Even if you avoid the trap of thinking that success means being like some other person, you might still have a wrong attitude toward success. Many people wrongly equate it with achievement of some sort, with arriving at a destination or attaining a goal. Here are several of the most common misconceptions about success:

WEALTH

Probably the most common misunderstanding about success is that it's the same as having money. A lot of people believe that if they accumulate wealth, they will be successful. But wealth doesn't eliminate current problems, and it introduces many new ones. If you don't believe that, look at the lives of lottery winners. Wealth does not bring contentment or success.

A SPECIAL FEELING

Another common misconception is that people have achieved success when they feel successful or happy. But trying to *feel* successful is probably even more difficult than trying to become wealthy. The continual search for happiness is a primary reason that so many people are miserable. If you make happiness your goal, you are almost certainly destined to fail. You will be on a continual roller coaster, changing from successful to unsuccessful with every mood change. Life is uncertain, and emotions aren't stable. Happiness simply cannot be relied upon as a measure of success.

SPECIFIC AND WORTHWHILE POSSESSIONS

Think back to when you were a kid. Chances are that there was a time when you wanted something badly, and you believed that if you possessed that thing, it would make a significant difference in your life. When I was nine years old, it was a burgundy-and-silver Schwinn bicycle, which I received for Christmas. But I soon discovered that it didn't bring me the success or long-term contentment that I hoped for and expected.

That process has repeated itself in my life. I found that success didn't come when I became a starter on my high school basketball team, when I became the student body president in college, or when I bought my first house. It has never come as the result of possessing something I wanted. Possessions are at best a temporary fix. Success cannot be attained or measured that way.

POWER

Charles McElroy once joked, "Power is usually recognized as an excellent short-term antidepressant." That statement contains a lot of truth because power often gives the appearance of success, but even then, it's only temporary.

You've probably heard before the quote from English historian Lord Acton: "Power tends to corrupt and absolute power corrupts absolutely." Abraham Lincoln echoed that belief when he said, "Nearly all men can stand adversity, but if you want to test a man's character, give him power." Power really is a test of character. In the hands of a person of integrity, it is of tremendous benefit; in the hands of a tyrant, it causes terrible destruction. By itself, power is neither positive nor negative. And it is not the source of security or success. Besides, all dictators—even benevolent ones—eventually lose power.

ACHIEVEMENT

Many people have what I call "destination disease." They believe that if they can arrive somewhere—attain a position, accomplish a goal, or have a relationship with the right person—they will be successful. At one time I had a similar view of success. I defined it as the progressive realization of a predetermined worthwhile goal. But over time I realized that the definition fell short of the mark. Success isn't a list of goals to be checked off one after another. It's not reaching a destination. Success is a journey.

THE RIGHT ATTITUDE ABOUT SUCCESS

If success is a journey, how do you get started? What does it take to be successful? Two things are required: the right attitude toward success and the right principles for getting there. Once you redefine success as a journey, you can maintain the right attitude toward it. Then you're ready to start the process. The results may be as unique as each individual, but the process is the same for everyone. Here is my definition of success:

> *Success is . . .*
> *Knowing your purpose in life,*
> *Growing to reach your maximum potential, and*
> *Sowing seeds that benefit others.*

When you think of success in this way, you can see why it must be seen as a journey rather than a destination. No matter how long you live or what you decide to do in life, as long as you have the right attitude about it, you will never exhaust your capacity to grow toward your potential or run out of opportunities to help others. When you see success as a journey, you'll never have the problem of trying to "arrive" at an elusive final destination. And you'll never find yourself in a position where you have accomplished some final goal, only to discover that you're still unfulfilled and searching for something else to do.

To get a better handle on these aspects of success, let's take a look at each one of them:

KNOWING YOUR PURPOSE

Nothing can take the place of knowing your purpose. Millionaire industrialist Henry J. Kaiser, the founder of Kaiser Aluminum as well as the Kaiser-Permanente health care system, said, "The evidence is overwhelming that you cannot begin to achieve your best unless you set some aim in life." Or put another way, if you don't try actively to discover your purpose, you're likely to spend your life doing the wrong things.

I believe that God created every person for a purpose. According to psychologist Viktor Frankl, "Everyone has his own specific vocation or mission in life. Everyone must carry out a concrete assignment that demands fulfillment. Therein he cannot be replaced, nor can his life be repeated. Thus everyone's task is as unique as his specific opportunity to implement it." Each of us has a purpose for which we were created. Our responsibility—and our greatest joy—is to identify it.

Here are some questions to ask yourself to help you identify your purpose:

For what am I searching? All of us have a strong desire buried in our hearts, something that speaks to our deepest thoughts and feelings, something that sets our souls on fire. You only need to find it.

Why was I created? Each of us is different. Think about your unique mix of abilities, the resources available to you, your personal history, and the opportunities around you. If you objectively identify these factors and discover the desire of your heart, you will have done a lot toward discovering your purpose in life.

Do I believe in my potential? If you don't believe that you have potential, you will never try to reach it. You should take the advice of President Theodore Roosevelt, who said, "Do what you can, with what you have, where you are." If you do that with your eyes fixed on your life purpose, what else can be expected of you?

When do I start? The answer to that question is NOW.

GROWING TO YOUR POTENTIAL

Novelist H. G. Wells held that wealth, notoriety, place, and power are no measures of success whatsoever. The only true measure of success is the ratio between what we might have been and what we have become. In other words, success comes as the result of growing to our potential.

We have nearly limitless potential, yet too few ever try to reach it. Why? The answer lies in this: We can do *anything*, but we can't do *everything*. Many people let everyone around them decide their agenda in life. As a result, they never really dedicate themselves to *their* purpose in life. They become a jack-of-all-trades, master of none—rather than a jack-of-few-trades, focused on one.

If that describes you more than you'd like, you're probably ready to take steps to make a change. Here are four principles to put you on the road to growing toward your potential:

1. CONCENTRATE ON ONE MAIN GOAL.

Nobody ever reached her potential by scattering herself in twenty directions. Reaching your potential requires focus.

2. CONCENTRATE ON CONTINUAL IMPROVEMENT.

David D. Glass, chairman of the executive committee of the Wal-Mart board of directors, was once asked whom he admired most. His answer was Wal-Mart founder Sam Walton. He remarked, "There's never been a day in his life, since I've known him, that he didn't improve in some way." Commitment to continual improvement is the key to reaching your potential and to being successful.

3. FORGET THE PAST.

My friend Jack Hayford, pastor of Church on the Way in Van Nuys, California, commented, "The past is a dead issue, and we can't gain any momentum moving toward tomorrow if we are dragging the past behind us."

If you need inspiration, think of other people who overcame seemingly insurmountable obstacles, such as Booker T. Washington, Helen Keller, and Franklin Delano Roosevelt. Each of them overcame incredible odds to achieve great things. And remember, no matter what you've faced in the past, you have the *potential* to overcome it.

4. FOCUS ON THE FUTURE.

Baseball Hall of Famer Yogi Berra declared, "The future isn't what it used to be." Although that may be true, it's still the only place we have to go. Your potential lies ahead of you—whether you're eight, eighteen, forty-eight, or eighty. You still have room to improve yourself. You can become better tomorrow than you are today. As the

Spanish proverb says, "He who does not look ahead remains behind."

SOWING SEEDS THAT BENEFIT OTHERS

When you know your purpose in life and are growing to reach your maximum potential, you're well on your way to being a success. But there is one more essential part of the success journey: helping others. Without that aspect, the journey can be a lonely and shallow experience.

It's been said that we make a living by what we get, but we make a life by what we give. Physician, theologian, and philosopher Albert Schweitzer stated it even more strongly: "The purpose of human life is to serve, and to show compassion and the will to help others." For him, the success journey led to Africa where he served people for many years.

For you, sowing seeds that benefit others probably won't mean traveling to another country to serve the poor—unless that is the purpose you were born to fulfill. (And if it is, you won't be satisfied until that's what you're doing.) However, if you're like most people, helping others is something you can do right here at home, whether it's spending more time with your family, developing an employee who shows potential, helping people in the community, or putting your desires on hold for the sake of your team at work. The key is to find your purpose and help others while you're pursuing it. Entertainer Danny Thomas insisted that "all of us are born for a reason, but all of us don't discover why. Success in life has nothing to do with what you gain in life or accomplish for yourself. It's what you do for others."

WE MAKE A LIVING BY WHAT WE GET;
BUT WE MAKE A LIFE BY WHAT WE GIVE.

Having the right view of success can help you keep a positive attitude about yourself and life, no matter what kind of circumstances you find yourself in. And if you can help the people you lead to adopt that same view of success, you can help them to always have hope and to become successful. Why? Because all people—regardless of talent level, education, or upbringing—are capable of knowing their purpose, growing to their maximum potential, and sowing seeds that benefit others. And helping people is what leadership is really all about.

But there's one more truth you need to know if you want to be a successful leader in the area of attitude. And you'll find that in the last chapter.

8

How Can a Leader
Keep Climbing?

Leaders have to give up to go up.

Many people today want to climb up the corporate ladder because they believe that freedom and power are the prizes waiting at the top. What they don't realize is that the true nature of leadership is really sacrifice.

Most people will acknowledge that sacrifices are necessary fairly early in a leadership career. People give up many things in order to gain potential opportunities. For example, Tom Murphy began working for General Motors in 1937. But he almost refused the first position he was offered with the company because the one-hundred-dollar-a-month salary barely covered his expenses. Despite his misgivings, he took the job anyway, thinking the opportunity was worth the sacrifice. He was right. Murphy eventually became General Motors' chairman of the board.

Sacrifice is a constant in leadership. It is an ongoing process, not a one-time payment. It's an attitude that any successful leader must maintain. When I look back at my career, I recognize that there has always been a cost involved in moving forward. That's been true for me in the area of finances with every career change I've made since I was twenty-two years old. Any time you know that the step is right, don't hesitate to make a sacrifice.

You've Got to Give Up to Go Up

Leaders who want to rise have to do more than take an occasional cut in pay. They have to give up their rights. As my friend Gerald Brooks says, "When you become a leader, you lose the right to think about yourself." For every person, the nature of the sacrifice may be different. Leaders give up to go up. That's true of every leader regardless of profession. Talk to any leader, and you will find that he has made repeated sacrifices. Usually, the higher that leader has climbed, the greater the sacrifices he has made.

The Higher You Go, the More You Give Up

Who is the most powerful leader in the world? I'd say it's the president of the United States. More than any other single person, his actions and words make an impact on people, not just in our country, but around the globe. Think about what he must give up to reach the office of president and then to hold that office. His time is no longer his own. He is scrutinized constantly. His family is under tremendous pressure. And as a matter of course, he must make decisions that can cost thousands of people their lives. Even after he leaves office, he will spend the rest of his life in the company of Secret Service agents who protect him from bodily harm.

The greater the leader, the more he must give up. Think about someone like Martin Luther King, Jr. His wife, Coretta Scott King, remarked in *My Life with Martin Luther King, Jr.*, "Day and night our phone would ring, and someone would pour out a string of obscene epithets . . . Frequently the calls ended with a threat to kill us if we didn't get out of town. But in spite of all the danger, the chaos of our private lives, I felt inspired, almost elated."

While pursuing his course of leadership during the civil rights movement, King was arrested and jailed on many occasions. He was stoned, stabbed, and physically attacked. His house was bombed. Yet his vision—and his influence—continued to increase. Ultimately, he sacrificed everything he had. But what he gave up he parted with willingly. In his last speech, delivered the night before his assassination in Memphis, he said,

I don't know what will happen to me now. We've got some difficult days ahead. But it doesn't matter to me now. Because

I've been to the mountaintop. I won't mind. Like anybody else, I would like to live a long life. Longevity has its place. But I'm not concerned about that now. I just want to do God's will. And He's allowed me to go up to the mountain. And I've looked over and I've seen the Promised Land. I may not get there with you, but I want you to know tonight that we, as a people, will get to the Promised Land. So I'm happy tonight . . . I'm not fearing any man. "Mine eyes have seen the glory of the coming of the Lord."[1]

The next day he paid the ultimate price of sacrifice. King's impact was profound. He influenced millions of people to peacefully stand up against a system and society that fought to exclude them.

THE HIGHER THE LEVEL OF LEADERSHIP YOU WANT
TO REACH, THE GREATER THE SACRIFICES
YOU WILL HAVE TO MAKE.

What successful people find to be true becomes even clearer to them when they become leaders. There is no success without an attitude of sacrifice. The higher the level of leadership you want to reach, the greater the sacrifices you will have to make. To go up, you have to give up. That is the true nature of leadership. That is the power of the right attitude.

NOTES

Chapter 1
1. John C. Maxwell, *The Winning Attitude* (Nashville: Thomas Nelson, 1993), 24.
2. Denis Waitley, *The Winner's Edge* (New York: Berkley Publishing Group, 1994).
3. Pat Riley, *The Winner Within* (New York: Berkley Publishing Group, 1994), 41, 52.

Chapter 2
1. Galatians 6:7.
2. J. Sidlow Baxter, *Awake, My Heart* (Grand Rapids: Kregal Publications, 1996).
3. See Luke 15:29–30.

Chapter 4
1. Proverbs 23:7.
2. Philippians 4:8.

Chapter 5
1. David Bayles and Ted Orland, *Art and Fear: Observations on the Perils (And Rewards) of Artmaking* (Santa Barbara: Capra Press, 1993), 29.

2. Arthur Freeman and Rose Dewolf, *Woulda, Coulda, Shoulda: Overcoming Regrets, Mistakes, and Missed Opportunities* (New York: HarperCollins, 1992).
3. Patricia Sellers, "Now Bounce Back!" *Fortune,* May 1, 1995, 49.
4. Lloyd Ogilvie, *Falling into Greatness* (Nashville: Thomas Nelson, 1984).
5. Genesis 40:14–15 NIV.

Chapter 6
1. Andy Andrews, ed., "Erma Bombeck" in *Storms of Perfection 2* (Nashville: Lightning Crown Publishers, 1994), 51.
2. Brodin, "The Key to Bouncing Back," *Discipleship Journal,* issue 109, 1999, 67.
3. "Where Failures Get Fixed," *Fortune,* May 1, 1995, 64.

Chapter 7
1. David Wallechinsky, *The Twentieth Century* (Boston: Little, Brown, 1995), 155.

BOOKS BY DR. JOHN C. MAXWELL
CAN TEACH YOU HOW TO BE A REAL SUCCESS

RELATIONSHIPS

Encouragement Changes Everything

25 Ways to Win With People

Winning With People

Relationships 101

The Treasure of a Friend

The Power of Partnership in the Church

Becoming a Person of Influence

Be A People Person

The Power of Influence

Ethics 101

ATTITUDE

Success 101

The Difference Maker

The Journey From Success to Significance

Attitude 101

Failing Forward

Your Bridge to a Better Future

Living at the Next Level

The Winning Attitude

Be All You Can Be

The Power of Thinking Big

Think on These Things

The Power of Attitude

Thinking for a Change

EQUIPPING

The Choice Is Yours

Mentoring 101

Talent is Never Enough

Equipping 101

Developing the Leaders Around You

The 17 Essential Qualities of a Team Player

Success One Day at a Time

The 17 Indisputable Laws of Teamwork

Your Road Map for Success

Today Matters

Partners in Prayer

LEADERSHIP

Leadership Promises For Your Work Week

Leadership Gold

Go for Gold

*The 21 Most Powerful Minutes
in a Leader's Day*

Revised & Updated 10th Anniversary
Edition of *The 21 Irrefutable
Laws of Leadership*

The 360 Degree Leader

Leadership Promises for Every Day

Leadership 101

The Right to Lead

The 21 Indispensable Qualities of a Leader

Developing the Leader Within You

The Power of Leadership

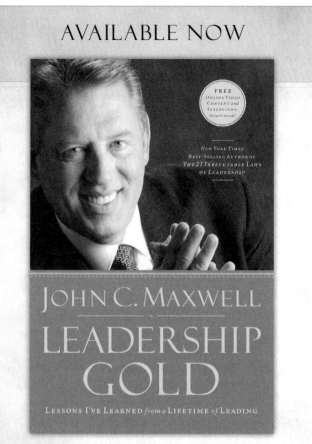

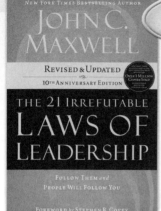

JOHN C. MAXWELL has combined his insights from leadership successes, mistakes and observations from the worlds of business, religion, politics, sports, and the military in *The 21 Irrefutable Laws of Leadership*.

Now, this 10th anniversary edition's additional practical applications and revised content make this book stand out above the best-selling original.

21 Irrefutable Laws of Leadership (0-7852-8837-6)

The Leadership expert, John C. Maxwell, brings an in-depth look at God's laws for leaders and leadership.

Includes:
• New articles and notes
• Revised indexes
• New interior page design

Available in hardcover and black bonded leather.

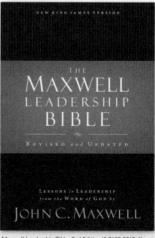

Maxwell Leadership Bible, 2nd Edition (0-7180-2015-4)

About the Author

John C. Maxwell is an internationally recognized leadership expert, speaker, and author who has sold over 16 million books. His organizations have trained more than 2 million leaders worldwide. Dr. Maxwell is the founder of EQUIP and INJOY Stewardship Services. Every year he speaks to Fortune 500 companies, international government leaders, and audiences as diverse as the United States Military Academy at West Point, the National Football League, and ambassadors at the United Nations. A *New York Times*, *Wall Street Journal*, and *Business Week* best-selling author, Maxwell was named the World's Top Leadership Guru by Leadershipgurus.net. He was also one of only 25 authors and artists named to Amazon.com's 10th Anniversary Hall of Fame. Three of his books, *The 21 Irrefutable Laws of Leadership*, *Developing the Leader Within You*, and *The 21 Indispensable Qualities of a Leader* have each sold over a million copies.